Musical Thoughts

Musical Thoughts

A Poetry to Ponder About

AMITOJ KAUR

PARTRIDGE

To order additional copies of this book, contact
Partridge India
000 800 10062 62
orders.india@partridgepublishing.com

www.partridgepublishing.com/india

Contents

1. Giggles of That Valley Girl

'Wow' was the word I said while looking at a valley,
In which a little cute girl was playing like a fairy.

Playing with sand wearing a pink frock,
And; observing people like a strict old folk.

I made my way to her with bare feet,
Nothing was hurting me but the sun's heat.

She said a faint hello to me,
And to become as her, I bent on my knees.

I gave her a smile which was pretty bright,
And she passed me a smile which was starry bright.

We played many funny games,
And gave each other some nick names.

As the sun was going to set down,
She suddenly started to make flower crown.

She put her crown on her head,
And picked her basket which contained bread.

She ran towards the vale's end,
And bid goodbye to me, her new friend.

I ran after her to ask her name,
But she suddenly disappeared and it started to rain.

I was astonished and thought of that girl,
And her giggles and her beautiful curl.

2. A Lonely Tree

I was standing by a lonely tree,
Feeling the essence of free.

I looked up and saw its leaves,
It looked at me with a gleam.

I gave it a shiny smile,
And it spread its fragrance beyond a mile.

It told me how my great grandfather played,
And story of an old man who sat on hay.

We discussed about nature's beauty,
And it told me about nature's fury.

It told me about my country's freedom fight,
And how man was overpowering nature's might.

We talked too much from day to night,
And my feelings took a high flight.

It remembered me about the greens,
When I went again I never found that lonely blossom's tree.

3. I love you.. ...

Flowers smiling, leaves shining.
And a rainbow in the sky.

Its nature at its best,
It never felt so high.

I can tell you really,
It's you on whom I can rely.

I now just want to say,
I want to fly through sky

I am feeling free, I can breathe free.
Now, I just don't want to cry.

I love you nature, I love you god,
Just always give me the power to try.

4. My Dreamland

Where the truth's river flows,
With happiness everyone's face glows.

Where singing is the way to talk,
And dancing is the way to walk.

Where celebration is everyday at supper,
And everybody is nature's lover.

Where breeze flows kissing the faces,
And one is happy in life's all the phases.

Where hard work is loved by everyone,
And just being successful is not all the fun.

Where rainbow of sunshine is our swing,
And a touch of colors with butterflies' wings.

Where with the rain's water,
Fun, happiness and giggles shower.

Where the trees freely swing,
With uniqueness, everybody's eyes bling.

Where air is fresh and purely clean,
And pollution is topic of only scary dreams.

Where atmosphere is aromatic with flower's scent,
And elegant tree canopies make our house tent.

Where sunshine is the symbol of our expressions,
And nobody is in depression.

Where hate and haste is just matter of stories,
And everybody lives in nature's glory.

Where there is no fear,
Where justice made is always fair.

It would be a place, which would make me glad,
And I would call it my dreamland.

5. Truth of the World

This world is too harsh but I cannot leave,
But this world is raising rudeness beyond my feel.
But I believe in playing and never quit,
Dear god, please make their minds fit.

Please, I cannot bear this anymore,
They say, "To me you are no more",
Son is betraying his mother, a sister too,
Please Lord tell them, good relations are few.

They are taking it too lightly,
No one knows to talk politely,
They are going to make it worse,
Oh God, "At least you don't curse."

I hope this world understands what I want to say,
Don't turn your lives into useless hay,
Love, care, share with everyone,
Accept this truth or from here, I have to run.

6. A wish in my heart

I am trying hard to fly,
To reach up to the sky.
I want to reach beyond the zenith,
Oh my goodness! It's too high.

But I can conquer it,
As long as my hope is fit.
How can I be so hopeless?
Therefore, I gave myself a big hit.

I will try with a hand glider,
And fly like a knight rider.
Through the sky with all my might,
And be as strong as an army fighter.

I will never let go, the twinkling light in my eyes.
I will try never to leave smiling at any price.
Moreover, I will never leave hope in my heart,
And, try it every time I lose, even if I have to do it thrice.

I will always spread my wings,
And stand among all the great kings.
But still with a wish in my heart,
That I want to fly through cloud rings.

7. An unusual dream

Somebody please remind me of a dream,
Where flowers were pink and grass was green.
Yeah! It sounds way too normal,
As if, the dream had rushed out from something formal.

However, something was strange about it,
Not everything seemed fit.
Something was unusual with fantasy,
Even fairies were not catching my fancy.

The rainbow stream flowing through flowery banks,
Rose shrubs made an elegant fence.
I had never seen a waterfall flowing upwards,
And never ever birds flying backwards.

Everything happening is crazy,
There were beautiful millions of daisies.
Something is wrong with either dream or me.
Thinking about it, I just scream.

Something is missing in our lives,
Maybe the happiness and all the spice.
Life is becoming dull day by day,
Break this monotony O' lord, to you I pray.

Because only smile gets noticed

8. Smile ☺

A smile, on your face,
That no one can erase.

Never let it wash away,
Even when your hair turns gray. (ha-ha!)

Let the smile wrinkles come,
Do not let a single tear from your face run.

You do not know how much I love your smile,
It gives me power to walk through tough miles.

Your little giggles, which can cool down any heat,
I want you to know that it is my favourite beat.

I love it when you are happy,
Because, that's what makes me happy.

Sometimes, you even go crazy,
But you are with me, nothing is hazy.

The only thing I want to tell you is that I love your smile,
And, I want to walk with you through all the miles.

9. Have you ever wondered....

Have you ever wondered why clouds float?
With airline speed, through the sky.

Have you ever wondered how a flower grows?
By breaking the marble slab and later its pollen freely fly.

Have you ever wondered how a child smiles?
It speaks louder than any miserable cry.

Have you ever wondered how waves move ahead?
Spinning and frowning when full moon is in the sky.

Have you ever wondered how a little worm,
Becomes a magnificent and cute butterfly.

If you have not wondered about this, then listen to me,
Do wonder why in your life, you cry.

You should wonder why you don't smile,
When a single smile can hold your heads high....

10. Cheaters

Oh! A rainbow in the blue sky,
I want to touch it but its way too high.

I want freedom from all the cheaters,
Called score, money, fame, oh these liars and cheaters.

They come, go, and fly far away,
And prompt men to spoil their day.

To earn them in plenty and keep them safe.
Men waste their lives and keep walking with a pace.

But when the time comes to test goodness,
Men come to know they have no true friends.

They(men) are betrayed, and cheated often.
Their happiness rests in cemetery in a coffin.

But these betrayers; score, money and fame.
Silly men still keep on working; maybe, they are vain.

After all, when finally, it will be the doomsday,
It will be only the god to whom these men will pray.

11. The little boy

I was wandering through the streets,
Watching people passing by,
Of every caste, every creed,
I didn't know what they wanted to try.

Then suddenly this little boy came to me,
I couldn't understand what he wanted to say.
Though I 'felt' what he said, it was a plea.
He requested me; for his sake, I should pray.

He talked with me through the language of brains,
It was the loudest voice I had ever heard.
It felt as if he was in deep pains,
It seemed as if he was an injured bird.

Whose wings had been cut with a knife,
Yet he managed to walk a mile.
He was swinging back and forth between death and life,
Maybe he was finding a reason to smile.

Then suddenly his nightmare came true,
He was shot dead in a blink of eye.
I don't know what he did, was his death due?
I think to date, that it was I to die.

That boy was humanity; innocent and pure,

And cruelty shot it dead in spite of my pleas.

I wish renaissance happens, because it is the only cure,

As it is better to have humanity in struggle

Rather than 'rest in peace'.

12. A test that moved me

That day is still fresh in my mind,
When I got a score which were not for my kind.

It was a science test which moved me,
And it was Monday and on Tuesday it supposed to be.

I didn't learn a single word for the test,
For, I thought it's on Tuesday and I should rest.

I enjoyed my Sunday.
I played and ate yummy sundae.

When on Monday, I went to school,
I again started to follow all the rules.

When science teacher entered the class,
My friends looked at the door, which had a stained glass.

When teacher started to give question papers,
My heart went down opposite the height of a skyscraper.

When answer sheets came back after checking,
I got two out of eight which were wrecking.

I couldn't believe my own eyes,
As my marks were always in the top five.

When teacher came back for seeing tests,
I was hiding my face like a bird in nest.

She called me and I went to her,
She then asked for my test notebook with words as soft as fur.

She rechecked my test and gave a smile.
(I opened it; it was seven out of eight)
I rushed to the girl with record file.

I was happy as if it was a big achievement,
And, told my friends about it with excitement.

That experience taught me about being happy for small things,
And not being sad and teary about tiny things.

Really, I was happy that day,
Because it was an amazing test day.

13. One day I...

I walked by a road, yes the rocky one.
It was tough, yet it was fun.

Taking every step on it felt like a roller coaster,
But due to which today I'm on every song poster.

Rocking a dress and electric guitar in my hands,
I heard people say there are my best fans.

Oh! When I passed a studio in my dream car,
My posters were all over; now, the Grammy wasn't far.

My every song was in the top ten,
Now everyone wanted to become my friends.

Everyone cheered up for me,
Not a seat in my concert was free.

I felt as if I had reached zenith, yes the top of the sky,
The airplane of my life's dream was flying high and high.

Oh! what a dream, I wish it comes true,
And I become one of those few;
Who are the best singers and maybe rock stars,
I wish that one day I become a super singing star.

14. Trampoline

A tree I was standing by,
Was a little bit too high.
I thought of climbing it,
First time; my head was hit.

I got an idea; maybe, it was crazy,
Now there was hope, and nothing was hazy.
So, I pulled out my trampoline,
But I feared it might tear as I wasn't lean.

Somehow, I took it out to the backyard,
Pushing it under the tree wasn't much hard,
On the trampoline, up and down I jumped.
My hope, through my every vein pumped.

I finally caught a branch, yeh! I reached up.
Now I took branch by branch, and climbed up and up.
Finally, I climbed the tree and was at the top.
All the fun and the little achievement was result of a little hope.

15. Enlightened by a train journey

Sitting in a train, by a window seat,
I was moving along the train's thundering beat.

Looking at the trees, seeming to be running.
Under the sun; happiness, they were churning.

It looked as if even the buildings were moving,
And streetlights with some music were grooving.

How pleasant, that train journey was,
Everywhere, I could see blooming flowers.

But something caught my keen attention,
Oh! I missed it; the feeling gave me tension.

After that, all through the journey I thought about it,
Nothing to me seemed fit.

But it clearly explained one thing to me,
A learning; that continued to live with me.

That, things in life go away rapidly,
If you don't hold them rigidly.

That, things just slip away from your hands,
And move away to nowhere lands.

I learnt that hold the precious things in life,
Or; you yourself know the otherwise.

16. The Angel's present

Every time I feel that, I am breaking down,
The hope angel in me, at me frowns.

She punches me hard and asks me,
"Why from tough tasks, you want to flee?"

I just hang my head with no answer to say,
She lifts me up and to God, for me she prays.

Then she gifts me something wrapped in love,
It's always good, pure and white like dove.

I ask her, what she has gifted to me,
She says, "When you open it, from sadness you will be free."

I untie the ribbon on the present,
After that, everything seems to be pleasant.

The gift she gives is probably the best,
At the bottom of my heart, then peace rests.

It contains perseverance, smile and hope of course,
It powers me up and gives me trying force.

Then I hold myself high with a smile,
And I get the power to walk continuously for at least a kilo miles.

17. A tree that wanted to grow higher and. . ..

I still remember the day, when that seed he sowed,
For tucking the seed into the earth, land he ploughed.

He pressed the seed into the earth gently,
And watered it amidst the breeze flowing gently.

After a few days, two leaves peeped out,
As if saying, "peek- a -boo" Oh! That was a sprout.

It grew into a big plant by the sixth month,
Pink flowers for the first time, blossomed on its front.

The person who sowed it, he smiled.
Now in the plant, his happiness relied.

He saw after some years, maybe two or more,
The plant was now a tree, it looked as if it roared.

Day by day, the tree grew bigger and bigger,
In spring, its blossom seemed thicker.

The tree was still growing very high,
It said I want to grow, until I touch the sky.

It said you should believe, "sky is thy limit."
In fact, you can go beyond and hatred! Just kick it.

At heart, you will be the best and most beautiful.
The sky will be beneath you and you will rule.

18. Something is going to happen

When the wind blows from the east,
It carries the sunlight's shine along.
Then the flowers prepare for a feast,
And I sing a merry song.

Then, songs were sung even by the beast,
And the flowers were singing along.
Now, the evil ones were in least,
And to make them good, it didn't take long.

I was singing a merry song, yet I was sad.
Why it was so, I never knew.
Probably everything is wrong with this cruel world,
As people smiling were very few.

19. Smile....Always

Smile always, even in your life's tough pathways.
It gives power to fight, till you get victorious days.

Smile in your sunny times,
And sing melodious hymns.

Thank God for he lets you smile,
Which makes your life worthwhile.

A single smile drives away all the toughness,
And if you smile much, it brings much happiness.

Forgive and make someone smile.
So that you live up to some more miles.

Smiling faces are like blooming flowers,
As, smile and flowers are true lovers.

Make someone smile, make their day.
And you will find, there your happiness lays.

20. Don't be.. ...

Don't be driven by fake smiles,
Because every smile hides a deep pain.

Don't be driven by the laughter,
Because people are 'showing' to be happy,

But their happiness is in vain.
Don't be driven by the tears,
It might be crocodile's and hiding fears.

Don't be driven by someone's luck,
Actually, they are unlucky to tell the truth.

Don't be driven by my shallow words,
Because every letter has something deep
to share about this world.

21. *"What's inside?"*

These eyes, which never let out tears,
Has an ocean within to let go.

This mouth, which never speaks,
Has an million words to blow.

This heart, which seems to be of stone,
Has many little-big feelings to flow.

These ears, which seem to be deaf,
Even listen to a petal's glow.

These hands, which seem to be doing nothing,
Has set many fields to plough.

These feet which seem to be handicapped,
Actually, to happiness, they want to run and go.

22. All about this world

Today, in this world where is humility,
In this world where is equality.

Everywhere is fear however no one cares,
Probably no one is so much dare.

Here is corruption; making the country weak,
There is destruction as terror is at its peak.

If I use any word to say,
Everything will go into hay.

I can better describe this world in very few words,
The words are 'sorrowful', 'terrified', 'dark' world.

Air is becoming impure day by day,
None can see now birds play.

Water is becoming dirty sludge,
Climate change causing massive floods.

Let us give Mother Nature her beauty back,
And try to see where in goodness, we lack.

23. Way to Success

I want to take a flight to touch the sky,
But there is a plight and I can't fly.

That sky of success with happiness,
This world of failure with loneliness.

I will break all the barriers,
To start my success career.

I will never leave hope at any cost.
And even during the storm, I will find the coast.

I will always step forward with little steps,
And never looking back will be my concept.

I will make a ladder with many steps,
So that my way is easy to success.

24. The Tree's Life

Those beautiful trees, Decorated the streets.
Now, the lampposts are the hosts.

Those large greens; with beautiful trees.
Now there are neither greens nor trees.

Those trees shined in the moonlight,
Then I was always willing to take a flight.

Trees give us fresh air,
And spread freshness everywhere.

They give us strong wood,
To make carved beautiful goods.

When these trees are cut down,
I am surprised that no one is frown.

Those greens who wore flower crowns,
Are now full with trees, cut down.

Think of the pain that a tree gets,
Like a fish trying to survive in a net.

Plant a tree every year,
Then, there will be greenery everywhere.

This will be a contribution to human life,
This will be a contribution to next generation's life.

25. Forgiveness

"Forgiveness is the power that I need,
Forget about the things that's what I feel.

Forgive me for the God's sake,
Because it all happened by mistake.

Now forgiveness is my need and not a 'want',
Otherwise, your tears will every moment haunt.

Forgive me please, even if you think; I am wrong.
Or the crack will become miles long…"

"Yes, I know it happened by mistake,
Oh! Please don't be sad and cry a lake.

I was never sad because of your fault,
But due to my strength's halt.

You don't even need to say 'sorry'.
Forget everything like a story.

I forgive you; yes! I do,
By the way, my smile was always a clue.

26. An Unusual Rush hour

During the busy and hectic time of rush hour,
I was standing by the road to go home, which wasn't far.

I crossed the road for catching a bus,
And carried my heavy bag, for which I had made a fuss.

Suddenly, I saw a rose plant growing there,
And many other flowers' clusters looking like a fair.

That rose plant had just one big rose,
It must have taken time, from soil when it rose.

Its blood red petals gleamed in the sunlight,
Its beauty lied above any mountains height.

Slight breeze moved its leaves and thorns,
Its faint voice was still louder than traffic's horns.

I was enjoying that rose's company
But then, my routine bus arrived.

I sat in the bus and headed to home,
But till today, for that rose I have strived.

27. Teachers

Oh my teacher! Oh my teacher!
You are my only preacher.

Every time giving me the light.
And helping to take success flight.

You cheer me up for every sail,
And also mend my wrong ways.

Telling me that every dark cloud has a silver lining,
And explaining that a diamond comes from a black mine.

You shape our future with gold,
The only thing you do is to mould (us).

In geography, you teach us about sea's waves,
In science, you teach us about sound waves.

All of my teachers, I respect you.
However, the words in my vocabulary are very few.

Amitoj Kaur